Remembering Our Heroes

Heroes

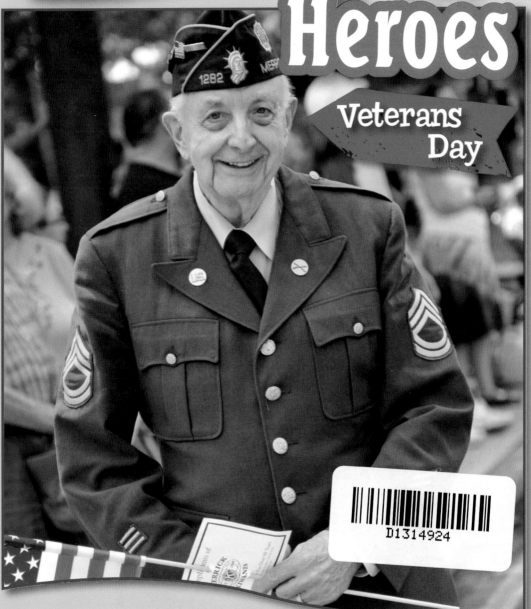

Kelly Rodgers

Consultant

Caryn Williams, M.S.Ed.
Madison County Schools
Huntsville, AL

Image Credits: Cover & p.1 Ann E Parry/Alamy; p.7 (top) Bob Daemmrich/Alamy; p.27 (top) Disability Images/ Alamy; p.4 (right) Image Source/Alamy; p.7 (bottom) Jeff Greenberg 4 of 6/Alamy; p.29 (bottom) Marjorie Kamys Cotera/Bob Daemmrich Photography/Alamy; pp.6, 19, 32 Richard Ellis/Alamy; p.28 (top) Shaun Cunningham/ Alamy; pp.26–27 ZUMA Press, Inc./Alamy; pp.24–25 Larry Downing/Reuters/Corbis; p.4 (left) Jocelyn Augustino/ FEMA; p.27 (bottom) Blend Images-Hill Street Studios/ Brand X Pictures/Getty Images; p.17 Ira Gay Sealy/Denver Post/Getty Images; p.24 Jeff Fusco/Getty Images; p.12 (right) AFP/Newscom; pp.22–23 (background) Terry Fincher/Express/Getty Images; pp.20–21 Keystone/ Getty Images; pp.9, 11, 14 (all background) The Granger Collection, NYC; p.8 (top) DeA Picture Library/The Granger Collection, NYC; p.11 (top) Rue des Archives/The Granger Collection, NYC; p.29 (top) iStock; p.16 (right) LOC, LC-DIG-ppmsca-08440; p.15 (right) LOC, LC-USZ62-25600; p.9 (top) LOC, LC-USZ62-47272; pp.8–9 (background) LOC, LC-USZ62-7456; p.20 (bottom) NASA; p.23 (top) Roll Call Photos/Newscom; backcover, pp.10 (left & top), p.15 (left), p.20 (left) Wikimedia Commons; all other images from Shutterstock.

Library of Congress Cataloging-in-Publication Data

Rodgers, Kelly.
  Remembering our heroes: Veterans Day / Kelly Rodgers.
    pages cm.
  Includes index.
  Audience: Grades K-3.
  ISBN 978-1-4333-7363-3 (pbk.)
  ISBN 978-1-4333-8845-3 (ebook)
  1. Veterans Day—Juvenile literature. I. Title.
  D671.R64 2015
  394.264—dc23
                                          2014010392

Teacher Created Materials

5301 Oceanus Drive
Huntington Beach, CA 92649-1030
http://www.tcmpub.com
ISBN 978-1-4333-7363-3

Table of Contents

American Heroes

The men and women of America's armed forces play many important roles. The armed forces, or military, protect and defend us from harm. They keep us safe.

There are five branches, or parts, of the American Armed Forces. There is the army, the air force, the navy, the coast guard, and the marine corps (KOHR). Each branch has jobs to do. The army is trained for battles on land. The air force fights in the air. The navy defends our waters. The coast guard protects our coasts. The marine corps serves on ships and on land.

Some people serve full time. Others serve in emergencies (ih-MUR-juhn-seez), such as hurricanes or earthquakes. Anyone who has served in the armed forces is called a **veteran**.

This soldier gives a woman supplies after Hurricane Sandy.

4

The 5 Branches of the American Armed Forces

Once a year we pay **tribute** (TRIB-yoot) to America's veterans. This is called Veterans Day. On this day, we honor all the men and women who have served in the American Armed Forces. Some people think that Veterans Day is meant to honor only those who have died in war, but this is not true. There is a different day for remembering them. It is called *Memorial Day*. It is observed each year on the last Monday in May.

Veterans Day is on November 11. On this day, we show veterans that we are thankful for them. We are thankful that they keep our country safe. We tell them that we are grateful for their **sacrifices** (SAK-ruh-fahyses). We express our appreciation for their service to our country.

Sacrifices

Sacrifices are things you give up in order to do something else or to help someone. Veterans make many sacrifices. They give up seeing their family and friends. Sometimes, they even give up their own lives.

Vietnam War veterans honor veterans who gave their lives.

This girl holds a sign to thank soldiers during a Veterans Day parade.

These Girl Scouts talk to a veteran on Veterans Day.

7

Armistice Day

The first Veterans Day was in 1954. But November 11 was still a special day before that year. That day used to be known as **Armistice** (AHR-muh-stis) Day. This day celebrated the end of World War I. People around the world observed this day.

World War I was a big war. Many of the world's nations fought one another. Many people were hurt and killed in this war. This is why people used to call it *The Great War*. The fighting lasted for five long years.

In 1918, they asked for an armistice. This is an agreement to stop fighting. It gave leaders a chance to talk about how to end the war. They agreed to end the war on November 11.

American troops fight in France during World War I.

World leaders sign a treaty to officially end the war in 1919.

Eleven

In 1918, World War I leaders agreed to end the fighting at 11:00 A.M. on November 11. That was at the eleventh hour, on the eleventh day, of the eleventh month.

World War I was over. People around the world were relieved. It was the worst war the world had seen. People did not want to forget this day. They wanted to honor the sacrifices that so many had made. Great Britain and France called November 11 *Remembrance Day*.

In Great Britain, people started wearing red poppies on Remembrance Day. This tradition (truh-DISH-uhn) began because of John McCrae. He was a doctor who had served in World War I. He cared for those who were hurt. He wrote a poem called "In Flanders Field." The poem talks about the many poppies growing on the dead soldiers' graves. These flowers are a symbol. They stood for sacrifice and hope. In France, people wore blue cornflowers. Just like the red poppies, these flowers had outlived the war. They bloomed on the battlefields.

IN FLANDERS FIELDS

In Flanders fields the poppies blow
Between the crosses, row on row,
That mark our place ; and in the sky
The larks, still bravely singing fly
Scarce heard amid the guns below.

We are the Dead. Short days ago
We lived, felt dawn, saw sunset glow,
Loved, and were loved, and now we lie
In Flanders fields.

Take up our quarrel with the foe :
To you from failing hands we throw
The torch ; be yours to hold it high.
If ye break faith with us who die
We shall not sleep, though poppies grow
In Flanders fields.

John McCrae

John McCrae

German troops march across Flanders, Belgium during World War I.

People celebrate Remembrance Day in Paris, France, in 1952.

In America, there were parades. Leaders gave speeches. They spoke about the sacrifices made by those who had fought in the war. Workers were asked to stop working to honor these heroes.

In 1921, America built a special **tomb** (TOOM). The tomb honors America's fallen soldiers. It is located in Arlington **National** Cemetery in Virginia. The tomb overlooks Washington, DC. An unknown American soldier from World War I is buried in the tomb. Today, it is known as the *Tomb of the Unknown Soldier*. To the west of the tomb, there are three graves. In the graves are unknown soldiers from World War II, the Korean (kuh-REE-uhn) War, and the Vietnam (vee-et-NAHM) War. The tomb and graves help us remember those we have lost. They remind us of the people who gave their lives to keep our country safe.

President Bill Clinton lays a wreath at the Tomb of the Unknown Soldier.

ARLINGTON
SILENCE AND RESPECT
NATIONAL CEMETERY

More About the Tomb

The tomb is made of white marble. It has three Greek figures on it that represent *peace, victory,* and **valor**.

HERE RESTS IN
HONORED GLORY
AN AMERICAN
SOLDIER
KNOWN BUT TO GOD

Veterans Day

People used to call World War I "the war to end all wars." It was so severe they hoped that it would turn people away from war forever. But it did not. It was not long before another world war broke out. World War II was even worse than World War I.

The U.S. entered World War II after the Japanese attacked Pearl Harbor in 1941.

General Eisenhower speaks with soldiers during World War II.

Dwight D. Eisenhower

Raymond Weeks was a veteran. He had fought in World War II. He wanted to change Armistice Day to Veterans Day. He felt that all veterans should be honored. He wanted to make Veterans Day a national holiday. Other leaders thought this was a good idea. President Dwight Eisenhower (AHY-zuhn-hou-er) did, too! He was also a veteran. In 1954, he signed a **bill** that made Veterans Day a national holiday.

In 1968, some American leaders wanted to make a few changes. They wanted to move certain holidays to Mondays. They liked the idea of making the holidays into three-day weekends. They hoped that this would let more Americans enjoy them. So the leaders moved Veterans Day. They made it the last Monday in October.

But many veterans did not like the change. They said that it changed the meaning of the holiday. Some states would not make the switch.

President Gerald Ford agreed with the veterans. So he changed the law. In 1975, President Ford signed a bill that moved Veterans Day back to November 11.

President Ford

U.S. Navy sailors

These people raise the American flag for Veterans Day in 1975.

Americans still honor Veterans Day. Every November 11, we remember those who fought in wars. The president lays flowers at the Tomb of the Unknown Soldier. We watch parades and listen to speeches.

Some schools take a day off. Others have special events for students. They listen to music. They talk to veterans. They learn about the armed forces.

It is good to celebrate Veterans Day. And it is important to remember what the day is for. It is a day to thank those who have served in the armed forces. It is a day to honor their sacrifices.

These students celebrate at a Veterans Day parade.

U.S. Marine Corps

One Veteran's Story

Many men and women have served in the armed forces. Their sacrifices have helped all Americans. Their stories fill many books. This is one of their stories. It helps explain why these men and women deserve to be honored.

Joseph Maxwell Cleland was born in Georgia in 1942. His family called him Max. They were **patriotic**. This means that they loved their country. Some of them had even fought in wars.

On November 22, 1963, President John F. Kennedy was shot and killed. The world was stunned. Some people were angry. Others were deeply saddened. Max watched the president's **funeral** on television. That is when he decided that he wanted to help his country.

Joseph Maxwell Cleland

President Kennedy

A President's Funeral

On November 25, 1963, President Kennedy was laid to rest in Arlington National Cemetery. Millions of people around the world watched the funeral on television.

Max joined the army. At that time, America was at war with Vietnam. Max volunteered to go to war in Vietnam. He became an army leader. But in 1968, there was a bad accident.

Just one month before he was to come home, Max was sent on his last **mission**. Max and two of his men flew to the top of a hill to set up a radio. This would let American soldiers in different places talk to each other. But while he was on the mission, Max was hurt badly. He lost both of his legs and his right hand.

Max was only 25 years old. He returned home. Over time, he healed from his injuries. Max knew he had to make a tough decision. He could do nothing, or he could do something to help himself and others.

Meaningful Medals

Max was awarded two medals. He was given the Silver Star and the Soldier's Medal for being brave in battle during the Vietnam War.

Max (right) during the Vietnam War

Soldiers board a helicopter during the Vietnam War.

23

Max chose to serve his country at home. He became a leader in Georgia. In 1977, President Jimmy Carter asked Max to help other veterans. He asked him to lead the Veterans Administration. This is a group that helps veterans. There, Max set up a special program. It helped veterans get used to life back home after being in a war.

In 1996, Max was elected to the United States **Senate**. This is a group that makes laws for our nation. He served Georgia in the nation's **capital** until 2002. Today, Max spends his time sharing his story with others. Max is a true American hero.

Max speaks during a campaign stop.

Barack and Michelle Obama walk with Max across the Normandy American Cemetery and Memorial.

Members of different branches of the military take part in a Veterans Day parade.

Remember Our Heroes

Our armed forces have been asked to serve our country many times. Each time, these brave men and women have been willing to help. They have fought in many wars. They have protected people in other countries. They have brought food and supplies to countries in need. They have protected Americans at home. They have helped during emergencies.

Each year, we honor these men and women. Some have served in the past. Others serve today. All of them deserve our thanks, but you do not have to wait for Veterans Day. If you see veterans, be sure to tell them how grateful you are for their service.

Two veterans shake hands.

These kids thank a soldier.

Share It!

One way to honor veterans is to share their stories with others. You can learn a lot from a veteran. Ask your family to help you find a veteran. Ask the veteran to share his or her story with you. Then, share that story with your family and friends.

A young girl visits a soldier.

This Boy Scout is happy to show his badges to a veteran.

Glossary

armistice—an agreement to stop fighting a war

bill—a written description of a new law

capital—where the government is located

funeral—a ceremony held for a person who has passed away

mission—an important task or duty

national—relating to an entire nation or country

patriotic—having and showing love and support for your country

sacrifices—things you give up in order to do something or to help someone

Senate—a group that makes laws for the country

tomb—a building or chamber in which a dead body is kept

tribute—something that you say, give, or do to show respect

valor—courage or bravery

veteran—someone who has served in the armed forces, especially during wartime

Index

Your Turn!

Time to Say Thanks

Write a few thank-you notes to veterans. Tell them how much you appreciate their sacrifices. Write about the fun things you get to do because they help keep our country safe. You can place your letters in one envelope and send them to the address below.

A Million Thanks
17853 Santiago Blvd. #107–355
Villa Park, CA 92861